Y0-IWC-301

RELATIONSHIPS:
Face to Face

by Carolyn Nystrom
& Matthew Floding

Teacher Edition

11 inductive studies
for students in
junior & senior high

Illustrated by
Joe DeVelasco

HAROLD SHAW PUBLISHERS
WHEATON, ILLINOIS

Copyright © 1986 by Carolyn Nystrom and Matthew Floding

All rights reserved. No part of this book may be reproduced or transmitted in any form or by any means, electronic or mechanical, including photocopying, recording, or any information storage and retrieval system, without written permission from Harold Shaw Publishers, Box 567, Wheaton, Illinois 60189. Printed in the United States of America.

All Scripture quotations in this publication are from the Holy Bible, New International Version. *Copyright © 1973, 1978, 1984 by International Bible Society. Used by permission of Zondervan Bible Publishers.*

Cover photo: James Ewing

ISBN 0–87788–722–5 Student Edition

ISBN 0–87788–723–3 Teacher Edition

95 94 93 92 91 90 89 88 87 86

10 9 8 7 6 5 4 3 2 1

Contents

Letter to Teachers

What are you doing with a room full of teenagers, a lap full of Bibles, and nothing in your hand but a list of questions? Not to worry. The Bibles and the students will do most of the work anyway. And the questions form the catalyst to keep things going.

A few guidelines, however, will help you weather your job as teacher in case things get more stormy than you intend.

1. Prepare ahead of time. A week or two in advance is not too much. Read the Scripture passage every day for several successive days. Go over the questions, writing out possible answers in your book. Check the Leader's Notes at the side of each page for additional ideas, then read the questions again—several times—until the sequence and wording seem natural to you. Don't let yourself be caught during the study with that now-I-wonder-what-comes-next feeling. Take careful note of the major area of application. Try living it for a week. By then you will discover some of the difficulties your teens will face when they try to do the same. Finally, pray. Ask God to lead you, as you lead the group. Ask him to make you sensitive to the students, to the Scripture, and to himself. Expect to grow. You will.

2. Use this studyguide as a help, not as a Bible. Students may use the blank spaces in this guide in several ways. They may work through the passage individually before your meeting and note their findings in the spaces. Or they may jot quick notes of ideas they don't want to forget while the discussion progresses.

In any event, the studyguide should never take center stage. Only the Bible occupies that position. So if you find that your students spend most of their time reading answers from the studyguide to each other instead of interacting as they study the Scripture together, it's time to ask them to close their books and use their Bibles alone. (You should still keep your guide to conduct the study.) Watch the eyes. If they are mostly on the Bible and each other, all is well. If they are mostly on the studyguide or on you, trouble brews.

3. Ask. Don't tell. This studyguide is designed for a discussion moderated by a leader. It is not an outline of sermons. When you lead the group (6 to 12 students work best), your job is like that of a traffic director. You gauge the flow of discussion, being careful that everyone gets a turn. You decide which topics will be treated and in what order. You call a halt now and then to send traffic in a new direction. But you do not mount a soapbox and lecture.

Your job is to help each person in the group discover personally the meaning of the passage and to share that discovery with the others. Naturally, since you have prepared the lesson in advance, you will be tempted to tell them all you've learned. Resist this temptation until others have had a chance to discover the same thing. Then, if something is still missing, you may add your own insight to the collection of responses.

4. Expect multiple answers. You'll notice that each study in this guide lists only ten to thirteen questions. If you treat these questions as a quiz (question-answer-that's-right-next question), you'll finish the whole lesson in less than twenty minutes. But you won't have done justice to the passage. Most of the questions assume multiple answers. Some even assume conflicting answers. So if your group is accustomed to a quiz format, you'll need to help them slow down and study carefully. Ask follow-up questions such as:

What else do you see?

Have we missed something in verse fifteen?

Do you agree with Doug's interpretation?

How does what you just said square with verse two?

How is this passage affecting the way you feel about Jesus?

When have you experienced something similar to what Judy just described?

Once your group gets used to multiple answers interweaving with each other, group study will become a natural means of learning. You'll be able to say less and less as they bridge the transitions themselves.

5. Always read the passage aloud—by paragraphs, not verses. Silent reading is great if you're alone. But in a group, distractions usually block concentration during silent reading. Besides, some students assimilate material better when it is read aloud than if they must use only their eyes to decode the meaning. And they will remember better what they *hear* as well as *see*. It's best to read by paragraphs. Verse-by-verse reading causes a brief pause after each verse and breaks the flow of narrative, thereby making it harder to understand the total picture.

6. Avoid tangents. Teens like to talk about a hundred things—not all of them involving Bible study. If you build a good relationship with your teens, you'll make opportunities to hear about the important things going on in their lives. But the purpose of this particular time together is to study Scripture and think through responses to it. So table the tangents and stick to the job at hand.

7. Pace the study. We've all seen the poster marked *Plan Ahead* with the last three letters trailing down the side of the paper. A Bible study can fail in much the same way. You work through the first five questions at a leisurely pace, suddenly look at your watch and then gallop through the last two thirds of the study in ten minutes. At the end you barely have time to spit out the application question, mumble something about thinking about it during the week, and then offer a one-sentence prayer with the closing bell jangling in your ear.

Or, conversely, you may quiz your way through the first ten questions, glance at your watch, and realize that you have four questions left and they need to average ten minutes each. Furthermore, you haven't done a thorough job studying the passage so the group doesn't have the background to answer those last four questions well anyway. Plan ahead! Each study should spread naturally over about an hour. Note in your margins what time your group should finish each section. Note questions that you could summarize if you get in a time bind. Note a couple of follow-up questions to spur further discussion if a question seems to lay flat on the table. But don't be caught leaving that all important application section trailing down the side of the page.

8. Talk about application. Each study in this guide ends with questions that encourage personal response to the passage. Some studies also have preliminary application questions earlier in the study. You'll be tempted at times to pass over these questions. They demand a certain level of trust with each other and at least some willingness to reveal personal thoughts. But if God's Word is a book to live by, a few people in your group (yourself included) ought to be able to make some comments about the problems and rewards of acting on its teachings. You should not bare your deepest needs, nor should you encourage your students to speak private thoughts they will later regret; the questions don't demand that level of intimacy. Simply encourage honest answers on a reasonably comfortable level. But don't skip application.

9. Pray for your students. Teens value relationships more than any other commodity in their lives. And they are forming relationship patterns now that they will carry with them forever. (Hate your mother now; hate your wife later. Defy your teacher now; defy your boss later. Scoff at the church now; abandon the church later.) Yet just when teens are getting these patterns in gear, changes in growth, emotions, and hormones make stability most difficult. The Scripture, with its millennia of consistency, can be their rudder during these critical years. Combine that with the mysterious avenue God has chosen to do his work—your own prayers, and you'll see your teens mature (slowly) into people sensitive to the presence of God in all relationships. You may even see God bring health into some of your own trouble spots.

Letter to Students

Dear Student,
God has written you a letter. Can you imagine it? A half page penned in silver on pink fluffy clouds pressed firm enough to write on, beginning "Dear Sue (or Mario, or Sam)," and ending, "Love, God." Wrong. It's sixteen hundred pages (more or less). That's as long as Tolstoy's *War and Peace*. Tolstoy spent seven years on his mammoth work of literature. Impressive. But God spent sixteen hundred years molding his letter to you. And he planned it from the beginning of time.

How should you treat this letter from God? If it were that half page of silver fluff, you'd likely read it with great concentration—maybe three or four times—then frame it as a personal memento and place it within easy view for all to see.

But God wants to tell you infinitely more than will fit on half a page. Will you ignore it because it is too long to read at one sitting? God chose to address his whole family at once, so that they could understand it and act on it together. Will you neglect it as if it were addressed to "Resident" and not to you as an individual? I hope not. A wise person will accept the Bible for what it is—all sixteen hundred pages of it: a personal letter from almighty God. In view of this, that same wise person will read it, study it, try to comprehend its meaning, and above all let it seep into the pores of everyday existence.

You are beginning a study of God's view of relationships. Relationships with other people—our need for them and their need for us—is one of God's good gifts. But he must have known that those inter-personal ties would take a rocky turn from time to time. So he set out guidelines in Scripture for bringing health to those scraggly links we have with the people around us.

During this study you'll talk about how to have a friend—and be one, what to do about needy "clinging vines," how to survive in your own family, how to reduce your chance of becoming a divorce statistic, and even how to look at yourself in your morning mirror. Most important, you'll talk about your relationship with Jesus.

A few guidelines will help you study God's letter. If each person in your group sticks to them, you will all benefit as you treat the Scripture with the respect it deserves.

1. Bring a Bible with you. Your own Bible is best. You may want to make notes or underline verses that are especially important to you. If you study regularly from it, your eyes will get accustomed to certain places on the page that you remember as significant.

Any modern translation of the Bible is fine. The questions in this studyguide come from wording in the *New International Version*. But we can also recommend *Revised Standard Version, New American Standard Bible, Good News Bible, New English Bible, Jerusalem Bible,* and *New American Bible*. If your church strongly recommends *King James*, by all means continue to use it, but be ready to make some mental translations between the English of seventeenth-century England and American language today.

2. Help keep the discussion on track. If God chose the Bible as his way of talking to you, it is worth an hour of concentrated attention. Be a person who helps the group focus on the Scripture, not one who pulls the group into less important, though perhaps more entertaining, areas.

3. Decide if you are a talker or a listener. This study is a discussion. It won't work if everyone just sits and looks at the floor. You'll simply wind up with a teacher who'd rather face a cage full of lions than endure another session with you. But a few talkers and a few listeners don't make a good discussion either. For a discussion to work well *everyone* needs to take part. So if you're a talker, keep mental track of how often and how much you speak. Then if you simply must open your mouth, use it to draw a more quiet person into the conversation. If you are a listener, pull all of your courage together and plunge into the arena. Other people will benefit from what God is showing you through Scripture. And besides, if you take the trouble to say it aloud, you'll even remember it better yourself.

4. Disagree, kindly. Many questions in the studyguide have no right/wrong answer. Most of them have multiple answers. So with all of those possibilities floating around, you are bound to sometimes disagree with other people in the group. Fine, disagree. You'll probably learn even more by having to defend a point of view against someone who sees it all a different way. But when you engage in these verbal battles, don't go for blood. God's letter is to all of his people. So when you disagree, do it not to win a battle, but to learn together and better understand God's true meaning.

5. Get to know other students in your group. Go out for pizza later. Date the girl across the table. Attend the school play where one group member has a part. Cheer the track runner at the meet. You'll find that a lot of interesting people choose to study Scripture. Take the trouble to get to know them.

6. Pray for other people in your group. Each lesson in this guide will have some questions where you talk about yourselves. These questions aren't intended to force people to reveal inner secrets. Instead they give an opportunity to think out loud about the way you are responding to God's Word. Use what you hear as a basis for prayer. A growing person, whether that person is sixteen or sixty, will keep on changing as he or she learns more and more of God. Support each other in that growth.

7. Memorize key passages. At the end of each lesson you will find a few words enclosed in quotation marks. These verses form a nutshell summary of the entire reading for that day. They are classic quotations you may even encounter in other reading. If you memorize each one, you'll have a mental outline for this book, and you'll recognize them quickly when you hear them in the future.

8. Enjoy your study. God never intended that we spend all of our days hunched grim-faced over his Word. True, it will at times convict us of wrong. And a grim face may, for that moment, become the most honest response. But Scripture also brings moments of great joy and sometimes outright laughter. Enjoy those moments with your group. And come away knowing that it was good to learn together from God.

Relationships: Face to Face

Your garbage collector, your pastor, your best friend, the kid who beat you up after school in seventh grade, your physics teacher, your mom—what do these people have in common? You. You have a relationship with each of them.

Relationships bring color to our lives. Sometimes the color is black, sometimes golden, and sometimes angry red. The colors blend, forming patterns jarringly jagged, or peacefully round; but without them, life is gray dull.

In teen years, relationships feel more important than anything in the past or even the future. In childhood years, relationships are limited by geography and by parents: "You may play with anyone on this block, but you can't cross the street." "Shake hands and tell your brother you are sorry, or you'll spend all evening in your room." And after the teen years, relationships are often dictated by job and family responsibilities. But during the teen years, a person is comparatively free to enter or leave personal ties, to nurture them or let them wither, to choose one over another. And during those teen years, relationships—particularly with friends, feel more important than at any other time.

It is just as well. Relationships *feel* important during teen years because they *are* important. During that period of our lives, when we are relatively free from other obligations, we form life-long patterns of how we relate to people around us.

As we might expect, God does not leave us to navigate such important waters without a map. The Scripture speaks in many ways about how we should relate to each other. It tells us how to treat a friend—and an enemy. It speaks of ways to settle differences. It addresses how we must relate to the needy. It talks about those who have authority over us—and those for whom we are responsible. It pictures the special relationship between those who belong to Jesus; but just in case we're content to lounge too long in that comfy environment, it also outlines behavior toward those outside the faith. And the Scripture does not pass over those most personal (and most difficult) of all relationships—those within our own homes. It speaks of child/parent ties and marriage and divorce.

But the Bible is not content to remain silent even after taking on these sensitive areas. One more area remains, one even more personal than all the rest. What is our relationship to that person we greet in the mirror each morning? What is our relationship to ourselves when we eyeball that image face to face? And once we've answered that question, we're ready for the most important question of all. What is our relationship to God?

1

Worth More than Rubies: Relationship with Myself, Part I

Proverbs 31

She's the girl with more male telephone callers than any other girl in her junior class. Why?

Sure, she looks good: long reddish hair, sparkly green eyes, slim build but not skinny. Her clothes say, "I like me." And her infectious laugh says, "I like you."

But what about her inner qualities? They will last longer than a few phone calls or a couple of dates. There's nothing wrong with self-confidence and good looks. But God expects us to be working on those personal qualities that last from teen years through paunchy middle age and even into the shaky seventies and eighties.

A long time ago, a godly woman gave some advice to her son (a future king) about the kind of girl he should marry. Proverbs 31 is the result.

1. What personal qualities do you look for in a potential date?

Overview

Superwoman. Today's woman hurls that name with a mixture of disdain and envy. Superwoman is the woman who gets up early, sews her kids' clothes, holds a part-time job, waxes her kitchen floor every Thursday on her hands and knees, single-handedly runs the PTO, does church work all Sunday morning with a firm-handed smile, and comes home to a well-prepared Sunday dinner where her whole family gathers at the carefully set table one half hour after they walk in the door.

Every time today's woman falls short of this ideal, she looks over her shoulder a little grudgingly at the woman with the cleaner floor and the shinier kid.

So when we come to Proverbs 31, women (and soon-to-be women) tend to bristle. Isn't this biblical superwoman a little too much? Surely the writer of such a piece never felt coarse brick floors under her bended knees. Or did she?

She?

That's right. Look again at the opening lines of the chapter. This verbal paragon of womanhood appears to have been constructed by a woman. True, that woman was a mother. She was performing the motherly task of giving advice to her son on what kind of woman he should marry. But that makes the proverb even more relevant for today's teens. Girls may well ask, "Am I becoming this kind of woman?" And guys ask, "Am I looking for this kind of girl?" And all of them wonder together, "Am I helping my friends develop these qualities that God values so much?"

Though this passage focuses on the qualities of a godly woman, encourage both guys and gals to interact with each question.

1. This question (intended for both fellows and girls) could generate a session-long discussion, but if you actually

continued on next page

plan to study Proverbs 31 today, limit your time here to 5–10 minutes.

2. Group members should discuss such phrases as "husband," "wife," "noble character," "full confidence," "all the days of her life." But don't stop with merely listing the phrases. Discuss how they contrast with today's common practice.

3. Your group should notice the many specific skills this passage lists, but then group these skills into general areas of responsibility. For example: husband care, clothing, food, business, family care, charity work, teaching.

4. Use this question for light-hearted relief. Don't attempt a thorough answer for each person in the question. But do encourage answers that reflect some recognition of the array of skills listed in these verses. You can assume that not everyone would like to live with such a person—especially if she were a sister.

Study 1

Read aloud Proverbs 31:10–31.

2. Look closely at verses 10–12. How is the relationship described here different from a "live-in" arrangement?

How important are these differences to you?

3. In what general areas is this woman proficient? (Look at the whole passage.)

4. Look again at verses 13–22. How would you feel about having this woman as a girlfriend, neighbor, mother, grandma, wife, or sister?

Worth More than Rubies

5. This ideal woman is skillful in a number of areas. What skills do you think are important for you (girls and guys!) to acquire?

5. Encourage personal s[...]sion. Your group members sh[...] feel limited to the particular skills th[...] "ideal" woman in the passage has dev[...]oped. Encourage both guys and girls to answer this question.

6. Study again verses 23–29. What reasons does her family have to praise her?

Describe the relationship between this woman and her family.

6. Focus on qualities that would command admiration, e.g. industry, self-confidence, and competence.

Use the second part of this question to solicit "feeling-type" responses as well as descriptive answers.

7. What ingredients would you like to see in a future marriage of your own?

7. The previous questions have provided the springboard for this question. Limit the "limitless" discussion that could take place about hair color, body types, and income levels. Instead focus on more lasting characteristics like those described in the passage.

The notion of developing qualities now for a future relationship may be an entirely new concept for your group. If the response is slow, direct discussion along the lines of personal priorities and what their effects might be on a marriage relationship.

Study 1

How are you developing personal qualities that will lead you to form a healthy marriage? (Consider spiritual, physical, emotional, and economic areas.)

Read Proverbs 31:30–31 again to see how the writer wraps up her description of an ideal woman.

8. In what ways does fearing the Lord relate to what you've studied in Proverbs 31?

9. In what ways are the personal qualities described in this chapter different from those that normally get compliments among your friends?

How could you and your friends encourage one another to develop the qualities praised in this chapter?

8. Lots of groups get hung up on any question that speaks of fearing the Lord. They ask, "Are we talking about 'shaken'-in-the-boots' fear or a fear that produces awe?" The Bible doesn't make much distinction between these two kinds of fear. In fact, it often lumps them as one. So if you try to define fear by one or the other dictionary definitions, you'll probably get bogged down in irrelevant semantics. Instead, let Proverbs 31 define its own use of the word. If fear of the Lord is a summary of this woman's character (and the structure of the chapter suggests that it is), then what she does throughout reflects and defines that fear. In view of this, encourage your group to discuss who she is and what she does and how that all relates to her "fear" of God.

9. Quickly review the qualities that the biblical writer found praiseworthy and contrast them with a list that your group brainstorms. There may well be some overlap.

Encourage specific responses that invite follow-through.

Worth More than Rubies

A Quote to Remember:
Charm is deceptive, and beauty is fleeting; but a woman who fears the LORD is to be praised. She is clothed with strength and dignity; she can laugh at the days to come. *Proverbs 31:30, 25*

Overview

We've all heard that "a word of free advice is worth about that much." The teacher and father who wrote this section of Proverbs had "spent" a good deal in terms of life experience. Now from his own experience and the treasury of Israel's experience the teacher was able to commend these principles to his son. It must have been good advice because today's young men still need the same instructions. And godly fathers today who sit with their sons and give counsel might well say the same thing.

Advice is never easy to take—even good advice. But perhaps the distance of the thousand years and the lasting nature of the counsel will encourage your group to make an up-to-date response. Again, encourage both guys and girls to interact with this passage.

1. Use this question to break the ice. Be sure to solicit a response from everyone who is willing. Try to encourage students to consider personalities that represent different aspects of their lives, e.g. peers, parents, heroes, etc. Take no more than five minutes.

2

Wise Counsel for Wise Guys: Relationship with Myself, Part II

Proverbs 3:1–12

Tim came from an interesting sort of home. His mother was a Jew who had become a follower of Jesus. Tim's dad was an unbelieving Greek.

His mother was understandably overjoyed when Tim made his decision to follow Christ. She and her mother (Tim's grandmother) encouraged and taught him, but Tim needed a male companion who shared the same faith.

Tim was enthusiastic about meeting Paul and developing a working relationship with him. Paul became something like a father to him and really helped him build on the foundation of his faith.

Tim was forever grateful for the fatherly support he received from Paul.

1. Among the people you respect, what personal traits do you admire?

____

____

____

Wise Counsel for Wise Guys

Read aloud Proverbs 3:1–12.

2. What structural similarities do you see in each pair of verses?

3. As you look through the passage, what reasons do you see for doing what the author urges?

4. Study verses 3 and 4. How are love and faithfulness *together* different from either of them alone?

If you were to carry both love and faithfulness into your close relationships, what effect would that have on your friendships? On a future marriage? On your relationship with God?

2. The peculiar style employed by the writer of Proverbs to present a moral teaching here takes an "If . . . then . . ." form. Your group should note that there is an instruction followed by a payoff.

3. Students have learned that there are natural consequences that follow from their behavior. Unfortunately the lesson is usually reinforced in the negative case. By contrast, the writer of Proverbs here focuses on the positive benefits of embracing God's wisdom in obedience.

4. It might be helpful for your group to begin by defining terms. What do "love" and "faithfulness" mean to your students? Your group might also cite examples of things that one can be faithful or committed to without loving them. Then discuss the kind of love that does not include faithfulness. After that, you will be ready to contrast all of this with the strength of love and faithfulness combined.

Your group will probably be more impressed with the "weight" of love and faithfulness in relationships if they discuss specific examples. These can be hypothetical or real. Negatively, every student can probably recall a time when he or she was hurt because a friend or parent didn't follow through on a commitment. But use these negative experiences to speak of positive ways to incorporate the learning into their own relationships.

Study 2

5. Again be sure that students understand the terms. If the response is slow, try one of these back-up questions:

"How can you use the intelligence that God gives you and expects you to use and still obey this?" or

"Do you think this passage places our understanding in opposition to God?"

6. Your students' applications should include concerns for humility and service. In the New Testament Paul urges the readers of Romans to think of themselves with sober judgment (12:3). He writes this in the context of concern for both individual and corporate Christian growth.

5. Study verses 5 and 6. Can our understanding cooperate with our trust in the Lord? How?

If you were to carefully follow this proverb, how would it affect the way you plan for the future? The way you approach knowing God?

6. Study verses 7 and 8. How does being "wise in your own eyes" differ from a healthy self-assessment?

If you were to consistently apply this teaching, how would it affect the way you relate to other people in your church, school, and family?

Wise Counsel for Wise Guys

7. Study verses 9 and 10. What do you consider to be your wealth?

If you were to follow this proverb, how would it affect what you do with the items you mentioned?

8. Study verses 11 and 12. What is the aim of God's discipline according to this proverb?

If you were to take this proverb seriously, how would it help you to let God be your Lord?

9. Take note of verses 1, 11, and 12. The teacher is directing this writing to his son. How do the instructions you have studied throughout this passage conflict with the image of masculinity encouraged today?

7. Your group's concept of wealth should include time, skills, intellect, and money. It may help your teens to dwell for a moment on the idea of "honoring" (v. 9) as they make applications of this passage.

8. God's motive for disciplining his children is clearly indicated here—he loves them. His aim is to have children who reflect their Parent/Creator and who walk in the way of life (Deut. 32:46–47).

This proverb begins to speak to a question your group may have already raised—not everything goes well for Christians. Sin and its effect on the world adds a difficult and dangerous dynamic to our lives. The passage gives the believer the assurance that sin will not go unanswered. We will receive the discipline that will allow us to respond in repentance and renewed obedience. This passage does not speak to the dark and evil things that befall all people, Christian or not.

9. Polarities might emerge in your group's discussion. How can we relate to other people in humility and service when we all know in reality it's a survival-of-the-fittest world? "Me first" doesn't fit well with honoring anyone else either.

10. A hypothetical situation is proposed here, so encourage everyone to respond. This question also provides an opportunity for review. If you feel it would be appropriate for your particular group, take a moment for silent prayers of commitment.

Study 2

10. If you and a friend were to encourage each other to become the kind of person described here, what would you do?

A Quote to Remember:
What you heard from me, keep as the pattern of sound teaching, with faith and love in Christ Jesus. *Paul to Tim, 2 Timothy 1:13*

3

Ties of Ribbon and Steel: Relationships with Friends

Ecclesiastes: 4:8–12
John 15:9–17

Steve spent the first three years of high school doing everything he could to make friends. He wore the right clothes for his targeted social group: faded jeans with T-shirt or button down, but no tie. He practiced the right language in front of his mirror until it sounded natural for him—enough slang but nothing crude. He kept his hair the right length. He looked bored in classes with unpopular teachers and laughed at the right spots with the popular ones. But whenever another student smiled and headed his direction, Steve's knees turned to mush and his tongue turned to lead. By the time he'd thought of something clever to say, the moment was gone—and so was the kid.

At home, when the phone rang, it wasn't for him. And when other kids gathered to study for exams or celebrate a game, Steve wasn't there. It wasn't that kids left him out on purpose; they just didn't think of him at all.

Senior year came, and once again Steve spoke to himself in the mirror. "Face it, man," he said. "You don't fit. You've given it your best shot. For you, getting friends is not part of the high school curriculum."

"Maybe I'm not missing that much anyway," he mumbled to himself as he turned away. "From what I see, friends may cause a lot more hassle than they're worth."

Overview

Friends: the most valued of all teen possessions. Possessions? Sometimes we view our friends that way, as if we could line them up next to the ten-speed bike and the high school letter jacket. Friends are part of our assets. They are good for what we can get out of them.

It's true that the Bible ascribes great value to friendship—it uses such metaphors as iron sharpening iron. But when Jesus talked with his disciples about his friendship with them, he talked as much about giving as getting. It's as if *being* a friend is what is important. For friendship (with humans or with God) does indeed create obligation. But Jesus made the effort to take his disciples into his confidence as friends. Then he instructed them to love each other in the same way. Perhaps we should do the same.

1. Use this question for a two-fold purpose: to outline the major facts of the passage, and to involve as many teens as possible.

2. Encourage expression of both positive and negative experiences with friendship.

3. Group members should list all the ways they can find in verses 9–17. Answers should include:

Jesus loved them (v. 9)
He gave them an example by obeying his Father (v. 10)
He gave them joy (v. 11)
He would give his life for them (v. 13)
He no longer called them servants (v. 15)
He let them know all he had learned from the Father (v. 15)
He chose them (v. 16)
He invited them to ask things of the Father in his name (v. 16)

Answers to this question should reflect integrative thinking rather than merely verbalizing the list. The disciples had been Christ's servants, but he took them into his confidence and made them friends. He alludes to the future cost of that friendship in verse 13: he will "lay down his life" for them. Yet for some reason Jesus *chose* these people (and us, his twentieth-century followers) to be his friends. In fact, as if to emphasize his initiative and obligation to them he says, "You did not choose me . . ."

Study 3

Read aloud Ecclesiastes 4:8–12.

1. In what ways does the writer express the strength of friendship?

2. Share one experience where you have benefited from friendship or have experienced helplessness without it.

Five hundred years after the writing of Ecclesiastes, Jesus was talking with his disciples. He had just told them that he was about to die. Then Jesus began to talk about friendship.

Read aloud John 15:9–17.

3. In what ways did Jesus show friendship to his disciples?

4. What are the obligations of friendship with Jesus? (Use all of verses 9–17.)

What are the benefits?

5. In reviewing the information in these verses, why might you want to become a friend to Jesus?

Why might you hesitate to be his friend?

4. Several obligations appear in the text. Among them:

We are to remain in his love (v. 9)
We are to obey his commands (v. 10)
We are to love each other (v. 12, 17)
We are to bear fruit (v. 16)

Benefits also appear. Friendship with Jesus brings joy. It enables us to love each other. Jesus causes us to be fruitful people. Not only that, we will produce a fruit that will last.

Regarding verse 16, "Then the Father will give you whatever you ask in my name," *New Bible Commentary* says, "*In my name* qualifies *whatever you ask*, for it must be in harmony with Christ's nature."

5. Encourage honest thoughtful answers to both sides of this question.

6. Expect your group to look at the ways in which Jesus gives himself to us and what he expects us to contribute to the friendship. (You've already discussed the passage in this light.) Then group members should think how that kind of relationship and that degree of giving of one's self might transfer into human relationships. Help your teens to think of specific ways and specific situations in which they can project the ingredients of their friendship with Jesus into human friendships.

7. If your group is small, assign one proverb to each person or pair of people. Larger groups may simply count off by fives. Take five minutes or so for them to study and make notes on their own proverb. Then reassemble and spend about fifteen minutes hearing a report of their findings.

Study 3

6. How would being a friend of Jesus make you a better friend of people?

7. Back to the Old Testament again. Proverbs are short pithy statements of wisdom. Select *one* of the proverbs below and write answers to the questions for that proverb. Be ready to talk about your ideas with the group.

Proverbs 12:26
Proverbs 17:9
Proverbs 18:24
Proverbs 27:6
Proverbs 27:9

What is the point of the proverb?

How have you seen this proverb to be true?

In what way can you put this proverb into practice this week?

Ties of Ribbon and Steel

8. In view of all you studied today, how is being a friend different from getting a friend?

9. Do you think that being a friend is worth all the trouble? Why, or why not?

A Quote to Remember:
As iron sharpens iron, so one man sharpens another. *Proverbs 27:17*

8. It might help to review the introductory paragraph to this study before you discuss this question. Being a friend may result in getting a friend. But the motives are entirely different, as are many of the actions. Encourage your group to speak in detail of these differences.

9. Most high school students have not reached the stage of giving up that Steve approached in the introductory paragraph. But they should take a clear-eyed view of the demands of friendship so they don't settle for surface relationships that they falsely name "friendship."

Set a tone of discussion that will also draw out the person who is tempted to give up on friendship, either because it seems unattainable or because an intense friendship has become too demanding or too painful. Be ready to spend some time individually with these kids later to help them sort out these conflicts.

Overview

Today's study contacts one of the touchiest areas of a teen's life: family. Not the lovely castle in the sky with handsome prince and cherub children, but the gritty here and now of irritable mom, busy dad, sniffly kid brother, and haughty older sister. The view of family, for many teens, is a game of gritted-teeth endurance until the closing bell rings at age eighteen, and they are off to college or a job on their own. Then real life can begin.

Scripture does not view family this way. It seems all of family life is related: parents to children, to wives, to husbands, to brothers, to sisters. It's not a matter of each person in his or her own corner, but each in a circle that joins and rejoins as child becomes husband or wife, and then parent to the children they once were. And the patterns of family relationships they form as teens stay with them from teens, to twenties, to middle years, and on. Funny that psychologists say much the same.

1. "Submit" evokes a variety of responses—mostly negative. Your group members should make their definitions concrete by suggesting examples.

4

War Zone or Test Site: Relationship with Family

Ephesians 5:21–6:4

Ted is a social animal. He fits well into his clique and is respected by his friends. He makes it to all of the social events, except when he's scheduled to work at Hal's Ice Creamery. He's often involved in decision-making for the group. Ted feels good about his ability to find mutually agreeable decisions with his friends through the process of give-and-take.

But Ted's parents probably wouldn't recognize "good ol' diplomatic Ted." He and his folks are often in conflict with each other, sometimes over the most trivial things.

And worse, no one seems able to yield to the other's will.

1. What do you think is involved in submitting to one another?

War Zone or Test Site

2. How do you feel when you choose to submit to someone else?

How do you feel when someone chooses to submit to you?

Read aloud Ephesians 5:21–33.

3. How might reverence for Christ help you to submit to other Christians?

4. What phrases describe Christ's relationship to the church?

How does the church benefit because Christ relates to her in each way these phrases describe?

2. If the response to the first question is slow, move to the second and answer the two simultaneously. Encourage your group to respond in feeling terms, e.g., relief from competition, fear of the unknown, responsibility and pride, affirmation, etc.

3. This question allows students with more Bible in their background to suggest answers including, "Christ came to serve, therefore we serve." A follow-up question that you can use if the group has difficulty is, "Why does Paul appeal to 'reverence for Christ?' when discussing submission?"

4. Be careful to include all of your students. It will be tempting for one student to give a complete list. Your group's answers should include: "head," "Savior," "loved the church," "gave himself," and "feeds and cares for the church." This question asks the students to place a positive value on each of these benefits. Encourage simple answers.

Note: The relationship of Christ to the church is crucial for understanding this passage.

> In Greco-Roman society it was recognized that wives had obligations to their husbands, but not vice versa. In this, as in other respects, Christianity introduced a revolutionary approach to marriage that equalized the rights of wives and husbands and established the institution on a much firmer foundation than ever before. One word summed up the role of the wife—"submit" (v. 22). One word does the same for the husband—"love" (v. 25). (*Expositor's Bible Commentary*, Vol. 11, p. 76).

Study 4

5. Suggest hypothetical situations that will allow students to formulate a response in terms of attitudes and actions, e.g., an argument, Mother's Day, housework, etc.

6. Resist the temptation to gloss over difficult responses. Encourage the members of the group to struggle with the passage and with their own values for marriage.

7. Use the entire passage studied thus far. Solicit responses from each member of the group who is willing.

8. Don't be satisfied with simply a rehearsal of the text. Press your group for meaning.

5. If a husband were to treat his wife the way Christ treats the church, what would you expect him to say and do and think?

6. If a wife were to submit to her husband in the way this passage commands, what would she say and do and think?

7. When you think ahead about establishing a marriage of your own, how might the teachings in this passage affect your plans?

Read aloud Ephesians 6:1–4.

8. What responsibilities does God give to parents?

War Zone or Test Site

What responsibilities does God give to children?

9. How can parents and children help each other fulfill these responsibilities?

10. Think over the past week in the life of your family. Consider one situation where people did not follow the ideals in this passage. Without revealing family secrets, what might *you* have done to help family members function more closely to God's standards here?

A Quote to Remember:
Submit to one another out of reverence for Christ. *Ephesians 5:21*

9. Paul writes in 5:15, "Be very careful, then, how you live—not as unwise but as wise . . ." Responsibility for the family is placed on the shoulders of each of its members. This question encourages students to live wisely.

10. Let each group member determine his or her own level of participation. An optional question that you could use is, "What else can you take from this passage that will help you to care and be cared for in your current family?"

Overview

Divorce is scary. The first divorce on the block, the first divorce in the church, the first divorce in your family—they all give a sense of wariness that causes us to look uneasily at our own marriages. Is divorce catching?

Scripture speaks of divorce in stern terms. "I hate divorce," God says in Malachi. Yet Scripture goes on to permit divorce, as the lesser of two evils, under certain circumstances.

But marriage—here Scripture speaks in simple beautiful language. And it gives ways and reasons to keep a marriage that endures. Perhaps if we paid more attention to our marriages, we'd have less reason to fear divorce.

Your teens can use this study to begin laying groundwork in relational skills that will later help them become enduring partners in marriage.

1. Your group's answers should include the fact of Adam's utter aloneness.

5

Forever Yours: Relationship in Marriage

Genesis 2:18–25 Malachi 2:13–16

Amy found herself on the horns of a dilemma. She had really looked forward to this Social Studies elective, "Marriage and the Family." Most of the material so far had been good and the small group discussions were interesting.

It was the presentation on divorce that made her feel uneasy. The approach was so—so casual. And the statistic that four in ten students in their district came from single-parent homes didn't help. It was as if being married or divorced didn't really matter. So—the dilemma. On the one hand Amy did not want to be judgmental about people who were divorced. But, on the other hand, as a Christian, she felt that marriage was something special, not to be taken lightly.

Read aloud Genesis 2:18–20.

1. Describe the predicament Adam found himself in.

Forever Yours

Read aloud Genesis 2:21–25.

2. Describe all God did to solve Adam's problem.

3. Since the events here outline a biblical origin for marriage, how would you describe marriage as God intended it? (Study especially verses 23–25.)

Malachi's prophecy addresses the issue of faithfulness in relationships. Beginning in verse 13 he discusses marriage.

Read aloud Malachi 2:13–16.

4. What words and phrases here help define God's view of marriage?

5. Notice each reference to God here. What does each suggest about the ways God is involved with marriage?

2. Far more than simply "make a woman," God took Adam through a process that demonstrated his love and care. This process also underscored God's concern that Adam fully value his wife. Help your group to cite specific details that reflect this love and care.

3. Answers to this question will come out of the group's careful analysis of verses 23–25. Responses should include: man and woman being created for each other, a cutting of some ties to parents to establish one's own home, intimacy between husband and wife, and a transparent honesty and openness with each other.

4. This list of words and phrases will help to "fill out" the concept of marriage as described in Genesis. Your group's list should include:

faith (14)
partner (14)
covenant (14)
one (15)
flesh and Spirit (15)
belong to God (15)
spiritual (15)
godly offspring (15)

5. This passage suggests a real commitment of God himself to a marriage. Your group's answers should reflect this personal commitment including his witness of vows, a sense of ownership, and his disdain towards divorce.

Study 5

6. God's hatred of divorce is related to the painful tearing of the fabric of relationships including those with God himself, the children of a marriage, and with the wife or husband.

Your teens should draw on their previous discussion and the text to answer the second part of the question. Besides the partnership being dissolved and children being affected, spiritual alienation from God also results.

6. According to this passage, what relationships are affected by divorce?

In what ways are these relationships changed?

7. Be sure that your group notes that divorce and violence are separate, despised acts. Divorce is itself violent because of the tearing effect on relationships.

7. Notice the words *divorce* and *violence* in verse 16. In view of the context here, why do divorce and violence seem to go together?

8. Discuss these verses briefly. Save time for application on the positive virtues of marriage and relationships. You might tentatively suggest that violent abuse be considered as another possibility for divorce from Malachi 3:16—"I hate violence."

8. Because human beings are far from perfect, God permits divorce under some circumstances. Read Matthew 5:31–32 and 1 Corinthians 7:10–16. When does God allow divorce?

Forever Yours

Note: God never commands divorce. He only allows it. Couples who work hard at forgiving each other may make their marriages survive even under these hard circumstances.

9. What differences do you see between the scriptural concept of marriage you studied today and marriages you observe in the culture around you?

10. Think again about the graphic way God taught the first man and woman to value each other. What could you do now to show that you value the people God has placed in your life?

How might this help you become a better marriage partner in the future?

A Quote to Remember:

The man said, "This is now bone of my bones and flesh of my flesh; She shall be called woman, for she was taken out of man." For this reason a man will leave his father and mother and be united to his wife, and they will become one flesh. *Genesis 2:23–24*

9. Use this question as a lead-in to the application questions. Because this appeals to something within the experience of each member of the group, draw in each one's observations.

10. Attempt to solicit a specific response from each member of the group. Application should be made not only to those whom we value naturally but also to the difficult people in our lives. The attitudes and skills that express esteem for a person in easy and difficult situations now may prove to be invaluable in a marriage.

6

Forgiveness and Reconciliation: Relationships in Need of Repair

Matthew 5:23–24; 18:15–22

Overview

"Love means I'll never have to say I'm sorry," croons one of the most wrong-headed songs in history. True, the girl was dying, so in this instance, the line might hold. But for the rest of us caught in the ordinary wear and tear of human predicaments, love means I have to say, "I'm sorry" a lot.

Scripture speaks often of the confession, forgiveness, reconciliation cycle. And it outlines ways for each person—the hurter and the person hurt—to initiate that cycle.

1. All of us have had the experience of having a "wall" grow up between ourselves and someone we care about. As students share their experiences of successful and unsuccessful attempts at reconciliation you might ask them how it felt not to have the problem resolved, or to have it resolved. Take no more than five minutes for this opening question.

"I never wanted to hurt him," Mike thought as he saw the pain of betrayal in Mario's eyes. Mario had never had a girlfriend. But last night after basketball Mario had confided to Mike that he and Shelly, the quiet girl in geometry class, had been talking on the phone and seeing each other a lot. "I like her," he'd said. "She has a steadiness that makes me feel like I've come home. Maybe," Mario had speculated, "maybe, if I asked her she'd go to the senior banquet with me. It's my senior year and I've never taken a date to a school banquet."

But now only twenty-four hours later Mario's eyes widened with hurt. It hadn't seemed like much really. Mike had just yelled at him from across the locker benches, "Hey Mario, did you ask that cute chick to the banquet yet?" Unfortunately his question had thundered into a locker room lull and now the whole team's eyes were on Mario. How could he make it up? Would his best buddy ever forgive him?

1. Recall a time when you felt you were on bad terms with someone. Was it resolved? How?

Forgiveness and Reconciliation

Read aloud Matthew 5:23–24.

2. What would be hard about making things right under the circumstances described in these verses?

3. According to these verses, how is reconciliation with a fellow believer related to our relationship with God?

4. Take a moment right now to think of someone who has "something against you." In view of these verses, what do you think God wants you to do about this conflict? (No need to tell names or grievances. What should *you* do?)

Talk to God silently about your strategy.

Read aloud Matthew 18:15–22.

5. Look again at verses 18–20. What indications do you see in this passage that

2. Your group's answers should include: 1) the public admission of need, and 2) the burden of responsibility for taking initiative in the reconciliation process.

3. Help your group discover that God desires reconciliation before gift-giving or worship. In some sense the quality of one's relationship with God is tied to one's relationship with fellow believers.

4. Be sensitive to the various group members. There may be some who are honestly unaware of any problems while on the other hand some may need the time to develop a real strategy for reconciliation. Your acknowledgment of the "poles" will encourage a more effective use of the prayer time. Without cutting anyone short, you might suggest that afterward you would be happy to give counsel and pray with persons who need that help.

5. The greater context for these verses is Christ's teachings on reconciliation and discipline within the church. The pronoun "you" in verses 18–20 is plural. God desires that the reconciling power of the gospel be experienced throughout the church. Therefore if all individual efforts at reconciliation fail, a group process begins with the full stamp of approval from Jesus himself.

Study 6

God places great importance on the group decisions of his people?

6. The roles have reversed; you now have something against your brother. This question helps clarify the difference and prepares the group for the application in question 11.

6. How does the situation described here differ from the one you studied in Matthew 5?

7. Have your group quickly list the steps. Focus discussion on the purpose of each step, emphasizing the positive value of each.

7. List the four steps toward reconciliation between two believers.

How would you describe the purpose of each of the four steps?

8. Don't minimize the pain of the process. Securing forgiveness is pictured throughout the Bible as a very costly procedure, including the cross.

The benefits of forgiveness might include: a greater awareness of being cared for, a heightened sense of commitment to fellow believers, a deepened appreciation of God's forgiveness in Christ, etc.

Your students' answers should include the realistic recognition of the risk that each step may, in fact, drive a deeper wedge between the two parties. Thoughtful students will also draw other benefits of an early settlement from the passage.

8. What would be difficult about the procedure for:

The person who sinned?

Forgiveness and Reconciliation

The person sinned against?

How could each of these two people benefit from the process?

How would each side benefit from settling the problem at one of the early steps?

9. What might Peter have been thinking when he asked this question?

10. If you were caught in the conflict described here, how would a conscious plan to forgive seventy-seven times affect your attitude?

11. In the two situations we've studied today, who bears the responsibility for initiating reconciliation?

9. Peter's suggestion goes far beyond the culturally acceptable limit (in Peter's day) of forgiving someone three times. He probably thought he was being very generous.

10. Use this question to prepare for the application in question 11. Draw out as many implications from the group as possible.

11. Whether we have wronged someone, or whether someone has wronged us, the responsibility for reconciliation remains the same. The burden remains squarely on our own shoulders.

Encourage full expression of feelings and opinions in regard to this important role. Be sure to pray for courage as well as sensitive understanding in seeking to be a people where reconciliation is valued and practiced.

Study 6

In view of the passages, why is reconciliation a difficult responsibility for the person who wants to follow Jesus?

A Quote to Remember:
How good and pleasant it is when brothers live together in unity! *Psalm 133:1*

7

Counting the Cost: Relationship with Jesus

Luke 14:25–33 Romans 10:9–13

It's a gray, early morning dream. A masked and cloaked man asks that you give him everything you own "or else . . . " With dream-like automation, you begin to pile your belongings together: your concert gown, your stereo, your books, your stuffed animals. You raise your eyes and silently ask if that is enough.

He shakes his head no.

You empty drawers: letters from an old boyfriend, old T-shirts. You strip your closet, even adding the Candyland game from kindergarten. Again you ask your silent question. Again he shakes his head no.

You travel to your basement and bring up your puzzles from pre-school, your baby clothes from an old trunk. Next you go to the garage, which adds your beat-up bicycle to the heap. Again you ask your silent question and again he shakes his head a silent no.

You stare at him for a moment and gradually you know what he wants: not just things alone, but people, relationships. Slowly you leaf through your photo album: mom, dad, brothers, friends. By now, more than anything else in the world, you want to please this masked man—you're not sure why. Slowly you close the album and add it to the pile. Again you meet his eyes and ask your silent question.

Overview

". . . by grace you have been saved, through faith—and this not from yourselves, it is the gift of God—," says Paul in his letter to the Ephesian church. "If salvation is a gift," we may well ask, "then what's all this talk about cost?" And so another paradox from Scripture steps to center stage.

As with most paradoxes, no simple answer solves the problem. In its most basic sense, salvation is free; yet in another sense, salvation costs. And the cost is high. It costs us everything we have and everything we are. True, Christ's death paid for all of our sins and true, even the faith to believe comes, at God's invitation, from him. Yet it is also true that once we have taken that step of faith, our life can never again be the same. We have given ourselves, our belongings, and everything we touch to Christ's control. He is our "Lord." This surrender of ourselves to God is not a payment for the gift of salvation. It is a result of genuine belief, an outgrowth of a gift already received.

Becky Manley Pippert in her book on evangelism, *Out of the Saltshaker*, tells about encountering a person ready to receive God's gift of salvation. She asked, "Are there any reasons why you should not become a Christian?"

> The person replied, "No."
>
> Becky shot back, "Then let me give you some."

A wise spiritual leader will point out the cost to potential followers of Jesus. Jesus himself did the same.

Study 7

He hesitates. You think you detect a smile behind the mask. But once again he shakes his head.

You turn away, sure now that you can never give enough. Your shoulders sag in regret. Yet one more idea comes to mind. Slowly, almost afraid, you place yourself on top of your belongings, knees doubled up and your face buried in your arms.

In a moment, you feel a strong arm around your shoulder. You lift your head, but you don't see a masked, caped figure—the mask is gone. Underneath is a handsome young man in the ivory tuxedo of a bridegroom.

1. Think of a time when you did not plan carefully enough for the cost of something. What happened?

1. Try to involve each person in some kind of response to this question. Group members are much more likely to participate later on if they get started talking early in the session.

Read aloud Luke 14:25–27.

2. According to these verses, what does it cost a person to become a disciple of Jesus?

Note: The word "hate" (verse 26) means "love less" (New Bible Commentary, *p. 911). See Matthew 10:37–38 for its use in a similar context.*

2. See verses 26 and 27. Then discuss briefly what each might mean.

3. In the Roman empire the cross meant one thing: the death penalty. In view of this, how did Jesus intend his disciples to view themselves?

3. Don't settle for a one-word answer such as "dead." Continue to probe its meaning by asking, "What kind of dead?" "Dead to what?" "How can you be dead and still follow someone?"

4. What would be hard about doing what Jesus says here?

4. An honest coming to grips with the commands here will reveal high demands. Encourage your group members to speak from their own personal values about specific hardship in meeting this cost. As the next paragraph bears out, it is better to anticipate the hardship and prepare to meet it, than to find it tripping us up by surprise.

Counting the Cost

Read aloud Luke 14:28–33.

5. Why are a builder and a king good examples of people who must estimate cost before they take action?

What harm would result if either of these failed to plan carefully?

6. What spiritual harm do you think might result if a person decided to follow Jesus as a disciple but didn't first weigh the personal cost?

7. Look again at verse 33. What activities, possessions, or people might compete with your relationship to Jesus?

5. Use these questions to help your group interpret Christ's two metaphors.

6. Your group should think of several possible spiritual complications: among them, false conversions with a quick reversal under the first pressure and later immunity to any invitation to follow Jesus.

7. Encourage each person to respond in some way.

8. See verses 9–10.

9. Not everyone will answer this question on all three levels, but be sure that all three levels are covered at some point and that each person responds in some way.

10. Your group should think of several reasons. Speaking about our faith forces us to clarify our own thinking in order to put it into words. This process may actually increase our faith. Speaking of our faith allows other believers to welcome us into Christ's family with them. It also gives them the opportunity to help us clear up any questions and to nurture us in the daily Christian patterns of living. In addition, a new believer is in the unique position of having many close contacts with unbelievers. To speak of new faith will allow these people the opportunity to make a similar choice.

11. Help the group to find assurance from verses 9, 11, 12, and 13.

12. If it seems appropriate, be ready to ask quiet people, "Pat, where are you in relation to this issue?" or "Jim, what

Study 7

Read aloud Romans 10:9–13.

8. What part must the heart and mouth play in salvation? (What must you believe? What must you confess?)

9. Think for a moment about your planned routine for tomorrow. If you were to say, "Jesus is Lord," and mean it, what effect would it have on your actions? Thinking? Feelings?

10. These verses say that we must express our faith with words. Why do you think it is important to talk about what we believe?

11. What assurance does this passage offer that God will accept a person who takes these steps?

12. Reflect back on both passages that you studied today. To what extent have you made the kind of commitment described here?

If you would like to deepen your commitment to Jesus, what next step should you take?

A Quote to Remember:
. . . any of you who does not give up everything he has cannot be my disciple.
Luke 14:33

are you thinking about personal commitment to Jesus?"

If this seems too much pressure during the group session, ask individuals afterwards. Arrange to meet later with anyone who seems to need further help in thinking through the kind of belonging to Christ spoken of in today's passages.

Overview

Paul's use of the body as a metaphor for the church is intriguing. For many in the church, including high school students, it seems entirely inappropriate. A church is, after all, an institution with boards, committees, and reporting structures. Impersonal.

And yet, Paul is insistent—the church is an organism before it takes any organizational qualities. It's within this organism, the body of Christ, that each believer has his or her niche and special role to play.

Again, there is an obvious discrepancy. The holy, exalted body of Christ is equated with a group of very ordinary-looking sinners. Our churches are full of them. This in no way diminishes the truth of Paul's words, "You are the body of Christ, and each one of you is part of it." Nor does it diminish our responsibility to live that truth out.

1. Encourage participation from everyone in the group. Each person has had some experience in groups, including this one. Clarify the term *diversity*. Perhaps the example of different body types performing various functions on a football team will generate some lively discussion.

8

Sibling Rivalry: Relationships with Other Believers

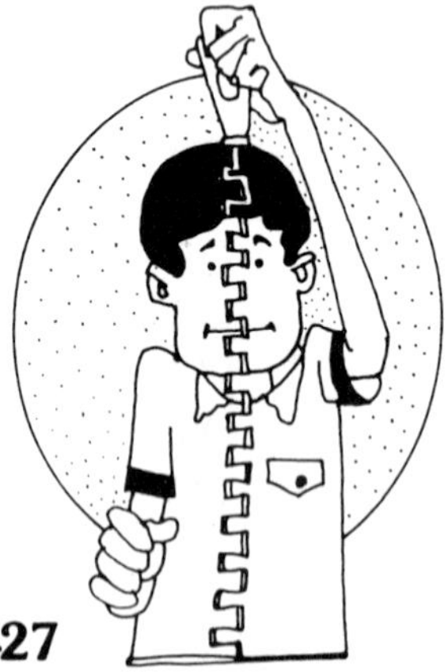

1 Corinthians 12:12–27

Judy and Pam have been best friends since sixth grade. They're both active in youth group, sit together in church, and have even done special music together.

Judy seems to fit in naturally. Her entire family attends the church and her dad is on the church board.

Pam feels a little bit of jealousy toward Judy. Pam's family doesn't go to the church, so though the people are friendly, sometimes she feels like an orphan. Youth group is better. But occasionally she wonders if anyone (besides Judy) would miss her if she dropped out.

How would you counsel Pam?

1. Think of a group where you have worked (your school orchestra, drama troupe, sport team, club, or class). How has diversity helped that group to do its work?

____

____

Sibling Rivalry

How has diversity created difficult tensions?

Read aloud 1 Corinthians 12:12–13.

2. What strong forces bind Christians to each other?

2. Use this question to establish the basis for Paul's discussion in what follows. Your students should note that 1) the quality of Christ's body, 2) common baptism, and 3) one Spirit binds believers together regardless of who a person is or was.

Read aloud 1 Corinthians 12:14–20.

3. Why do you think Paul chose the picture of a human body to show how Christians relate to each other?

3. Be sure to draw upon the entire passage for this question.

4. Why might a believer feel that he or she did not fit well into the body?

4. You may wish to encourage members of your group to share personal experiences of times when they felt they didn't fit.

5. What have you seen in the passage so far that would encourage you to maintain a relationship with Christians, even if you didn't feel very similar to them?

5. Your group should spot phrases that affirm the value of each member and God's sovereignty over the body, as in verses 15, 16, and 18.

Study 8

Read aloud verses 21–27.

6. Paul begins speaking of the various parts in verse 22. Be sure that your group cites the four categories specifically. They should find: 1) weaker, 2) less honorable, 3) unpresentable, and 4) presentable. Help keep your group from being hung up on physical body parts and to focus on the spiritual body of Christ, his people.

Using these categories, encourage your group to paint a realistic picture. What Paul describes here is not a patronizing attitude but the honest recognition that there are believers who need special treatment. There are believers, for example, who are mentally disturbed.

Keep your group rooted in the passage to answer this. Paul says the church is to treat 1) the weaker as indispensable, 2) the less honorable with special honor, 3) the unpresentable with special modesty and 4) the presentable with no special treatment. Use this question to prepare group members to express their personal opinion in the next question.

7. Encourage all of the group members to participate in brainstorming applications.

8. Use all of the passage to answer this question. The statement "I don't need you" comes from verse 21. If the response is slow, move to the next part of the question and answer both simultaneously.

Again, encourage teens to pick up on Paul's phrases and images to support their answers.

6. What four descriptive categories does Paul use to describe the various parts of the body?

Describe the kind of Christians that you think might fit into these categories.

How does Paul say Christians should treat each of these kinds of believers?

7. In what practical ways could a group of Christians carry out these commands?

8. Why is it wrong to think, "I don't need you" about another believer?

Why is it equally wrong to think, "They don't need me"?

9. Take a few moments to thoughtfully look back through today's study. Write one change you would like to bring about in your relationship with Christians.

If you would like, tell your group about this.

A Quote to Remember:
Now you are the body of Christ, and each one of you is part of it. *1 Corinthians 12:27*

9. Avoid pressuring students into making empty commitments. Allow for those who will write a response but prefer not to share. Some, on the other hand, may be genuinely led to address real hurts and needs within the group. During the group's closing prayer some students may wish to "seal" their commitments. Be sensitive to this opportunity.

9

On Mission from God: Relationships with the World

John 17:1–19

Jill attends a Christian school and a Bible-teaching church. After school, she works as a waitress in a restaurant run by Christians. Her school choir sings sacred music, and her school drama department puts on gospel plays. Her family is Christian and so are all her friends, though some place themselves a little reluctantly in that fold. If she thinks about it, Jill hasn't had a long conversation with a non-believer in years.

Mike attends public school and works at a car repair shop after school. (No Christians there, as far as he knows.) He plays basketball and also works as assistant editor for the school newspaper. He hasn't bumped into any Christian in those groups either. Mike also goes to church, the same church as Jill.

Mike has two sets of friends. On Sundays, he sees his Christian friends—the kids from church. He even goes with them for occasional special events or retreats. But the rest of the time he spends with kids from school or the neighborhood or the newspaper staff or the basketball team. And they don't even know that Mike's a Christian. The subject just never comes up.

Both Jill and Mike are Christians. And they live in the same world. But neither has found the kind of relationship with that world that Jesus expects of his followers.

Overview

"Where is home?" I asked my friend, Carol. Carol had grown up as a missionary kid in South America. Then she went to college in the U.S., but soon departed to Africa with a husband and children to do mission work of her own. Eventually, she wound up in the American Midwest. Understandably, she sometimes felt out of sync with the tree-lined sameness of a college town. Carol had no answer to my question. After a moment of confused silence, her husband came to the rescue with a big grin and the quote, "This world is not my home."

Though Carol's feelings of displacement may be more pronounced than those of most Christians, they are a healthy sign of spiritual integrity. Jesus spoke of this tension when he prayed for his disciples. He described them as "in the world but not of it." Like ET, home is far away.

Yet Jesus did not ask that God separate his chosen few from the alien forces around them. Instead, Jesus referred to his own work in the world—the work his people are to carry on.

On Mission from God

1. How is a Christian different from other people?

1. Your group members should point out a wide array of differences, not necessarily agreeing with each other. Try to avoid legalistic tangents. Use this question to introduce the subject of Christian distinctives. You can refine these later in the study. Try to involve each person with this question.

Read aloud John 17:1–5.

2. According to this part of Christ's prayer, how does eternal life relate to Jesus?

2. See verses 2 and 3.

3. How would you define the word *glory* from the way it is used here?

3. Use this question to continue exploring the first five verses of Christ's prayer. You may not agree about a definition of the word *glory*, but discussing its varied uses will encourage closer examination of the passage. (*Glory* also appears in verse 10.)

Read aloud John 17:6–19.

4. What is the believer's relationship to the world? (Examine carefully verses 6–8, 14, and 17.)

Note: Word may have several meanings here. 1) Old Testament Scriptures. 2) Christ's teachings. 3) A combination of the Old Testament and the teachings of Jesus. 4) Christ himself.

4. This is a convoluted section of Scripture. Help your teens do careful study of verses 6–8, 14, and 17 in order to prepare for the next questions. The definitions of "word" may help them understand what Christ meant.

Study 9

5. See verses 5, 6, 9, 11, 13, 14, 15, 16, 18.

Note: Verse 12, "None has been lost except the one doomed to destruction so that Scripture would be fulfilled." A comparison of Psalm 41:9 with John 13:18 will show that these words refer to Judas.

5. Mark in your Bible each use of the word *world*. What does each one suggest about the believer's relationship with the world?

6. Use this question to study more carefully these final verses.

6. In what ways is the believer's relationship to the world tied to Christ's relationship to the world (verses 13–19)?

7, 8. If your group members have done their work, they have spent a long time with heads bent over the text. Draw on your study of the passage as you discuss these questions, but expect the heads to pop up as people talk with each other about their own experiences with Christ's teachings here.

7. Why should a follower of Jesus expect to not fit easily into the world?

8. When has your commitment to follow Jesus conflicted with your desire to "fit in"?

On Mission from God

9. What kinds of protection does a person who follows Jesus need? (See especially verses 11, 12, and 15.)

What forms might this protection take?

10. Look again at verses 16–19. Jesus says he has sent his disciples into the world. Yet in the next verse, he says they are sanctified or set apart. In view of Christ's purpose in the world, what are his followers supposed to do?

11. Choose one of your answers to question 10. In what way could you apply this insight to a situation you will face this week?

A Quote to Remember:
Therefore go and make disciples of all nations, baptizing them in the name of the Father and of the Son and of the Holy Spirit, and teaching them to obey everything I have commanded you. And surely I am with you always, to the very end of the age. *Matthew 28:19–20*

9. People who follow Jesus need many kinds of protection. The passage hints at some of these. They may need protection from the world, protection from doubts, protection from Satan (verse 15), protection from their desires to be accepted in both the believing and the unbelieving world.

Discuss forms of protection implied by the passage. Believers bear the name *Christian*. They have the protection of Christ's name (verse 11). They also have the Word, with all its meanings. (See note page 51.) Believers also have the protection of Christian unity described in verse 11. Teens in your group may also discuss the protections of their own experience: family, church, believing friends.

10. Your group should draw on its discussion of Christ's work today as it interprets these final verses. But if the ideas of following Jesus in a relationship with the world lean too heavily toward the non-threatening, ask teens if their ideas would call for the protection described in the passage. For a synopsis of Christ's purpose in the world, see verses 2–4.

11. For an alternative way to close your study, try this question: Think back to the situation that came to your mind when you discussed question 8. How could you represent Christ in that setting?

10

Lemons and Liabilities: Relationships with the Needy

Luke 10:25–37

Kim's friend Glenda is a liability. Glenda became a Christian a couple of years ago through an after-school club, and ever since, she's been counting on the Christians there, including Kim, to take care of her.

Glenda's parents split years ago. Her mom works in a factory during the week and bar-hops all weekend. She hops from manfriend to manfriend almost as frequently.

Glenda goes through phases when she covers the party scene pretty heavily herself. Sometimes she calls Kim when she's too drunk to drive home. And her choice of boyfriends leans toward the unsavory. She's always asking Kim's advice on some impossible boy problem. As for school work, she studies hard but only in spurts. And even when she's working, the grades don't come easily. If Kim agrees to study with her the night before an exam, she feels stuck with a tutoring job—not a joint cram session.

Still Glenda keeps calling herself a Christian. She talks about how much Jesus Christ means to her and how much she needs her new Christian friends. But Kim just feels used. What should she do?

Overview

"The hottest places in hell are reserved for those who, in the face of moral crisis, retain a place of neutrality," wrote Dante in his *Inferno*.

Jesus spoke the same language in his parable of the Good Samaritan. He used it when an expert in religious law approached him with a test question. The lawyer asked an academic question and expected an academic answer. He got his answer, but it was not couched in the scholarly language he wanted. Instead of "Think this," or, "Believe that," Jesus said that awful demanding word, "Do."

It's an easy temptation for students of this passage to fall into the same pattern of the lawyer. We want to know how we should *feel* toward the needy. We want to develop a *philosophy* of service. But Jesus settles for no such armchair acquiescence. His parable teaches action.

Help your group, as you study together, to express thoughts and feelings that move forward toward action. The needy around us aren't served by warm fuzzy feelings.

Lemons and Liabilities

1. What kinds of needs do you see in the people who touch your life?

Read aloud Luke 10:25–29.

2. In what ways did Jesus and the lawyer agree about the Law?

Note: "The Law" refers to God's instructions for right living, summarized in the Ten Commandments. Sometimes it refers to all of the Old Testament writings.

How does their conversation unveil each one's relationship to the Law?

3. Why didn't Jesus say in verse 28, "Feel this way and you will live"?

1. Encourage each person to respond at least briefly to this question. Teens will be more likely to participate in the more difficult questions later in the study if they chime in on a less threatening question now.

2. Verse 27 forms an obvious answer, but don't stop with that. Both Jesus and the lawyer accepted the Law as authority. And they both knew the Law well enough to know that this particular law (Deut. 6:5 and Lev. 19:18) was a summary of its content.

Did Jesus and the lawyer agree that a person can inherit eternal life by obeying the Law? Some of your group may think so, particularly in view of verse 28. But has anyone, except Christ himself, ever fully obeyed the Law? The ensuing parable gives only a small example of the demands of this simple definition of love.

Be sure your teens speak of both Jesus and the lawyer in their answers to the second question. The lawyer saw the Law as a means to test Jesus. He also wanted to use it to inherit eternal life. (See verse 25.) He wanted to use the Law to justify himself. He seemed to want to escape acting on his knowledge of the Law.

Christ, on the other hand, saw the Law as valid too. He was in no sense wiping it out. But he saw the Law as demanding *action*. Christ taught the Law, but taught it in the form of work as well as thought.

3. We often think of love as a feeling, but the emphasis throughout this passage is on action. (The word *do* appears in verses 25, 28, and 37.)) Help your group to see the contrast between the usual interpretation of love and Christ's definition. The actions of love become even more significant in the parable to follow.

Study 10

Read aloud Luke 10:29–37.

4. Compare the lawyer's question in verse 29 with Christ's question in verse 36. What different emphasis do you see?

4. Use this question to study these verses more carefully.

5. Do you see the priest and Levite as unusually cruel or as rather normal? Why?

5. Expect answers from both sides of this question. Help students to interact with each other's ideas as they discuss this. Don't feel that you must jump in to settle the disagreement. Help them to focus their attention on the Scripture and on each other—not on the discussion leader.

6. What actions show the degree of the Samaritan's compassion for the injured man?

6. Verses 33–35 list nine ways the Samaritan cared for this man. Your group should name these actions, taking note of the unusual degree of commitment to help. For example, "I will reimburse you for any extra expense." (v. 35) is virtually a blank check to the innkeeper and to the victim himself. The Samaritan's response was far more than a token assent to the command to love.

7. If the lawyer decided to benefit all that he could from his encounter with Jesus, what could he have learned?

7. Use this question to help your group interpret the entire passage. Several different ideas about all this lawyer could have learned should emerge from your discussion.

Lemons and Liabilities

8. What qualities in the Samaritan do you admire?

9. Recall the needs you talked about at the beginning of the study. If you were to imitate the Samaritan, how would your attitude change toward people in need?

10. Focus on one need that you mentioned. If you chose to follow the Samaritan's example, what all would you do to meet that need?

A Quote to Remember:
Dear children, let us not love with words or tongue but with actions and in truth.
1 John 3:18

8. Discussion here should not be a repeat of question 6. Use the actions you noted there to reveal the personality of the Samaritan. Group members should then mention those personal qualities they would like to emulate.

9, 10. Save about ten minutes of your time together to discuss these application questions in an unhurried manner. It would hardly be appropriate to leave a study where Christ's main emphasis is action, with no more than an intellectual idea of what the Scripture means. Encourage as many as are willing to speak of an attitude change that would move on to specific action.

11

Sandpaper and Porcupines: Relationships with Ordinary People

Romans 12:9–21

Overview

You've reached the end of your study of relationships. You've studied what Scripture says about relating to ourselves, to our families, our friends, believers, unbelievers, the needy—and even how we can relate to God. This final study from Romans 12 is an umbrella study. It lays down general principles for relationships, whether they are with the comparatively easy "sandpaper" people of our lives or the more difficult "porcupines." Paul even uses the term "enemies."

The apostle brackets this section of his letter to the church at Rome with two great stabilizing principles. He begins, "Love must be sincere," and he ends, "Do not be overcome with evil, but overcome evil with good." Each person we touch will benefit if we live out those commands.

"How do porcupines hug?" goes the old joke. Answer: "Very carefully."

Some of the people in our relationships are porcupines—and we may grow a few quills of our own when we respond to them. There's Aunt Sue who can turn the safest comment into an imagined insult. There's your friend Steve who runs an air-tight schedule of sports, studies, and work—and jumps if you accidentally poke him in the back. When you talk with him, you feel like his mind is already rushing off to his next project. Then there's your sister Andrea. She's fourteen and itching for a fight—always. If there's no reason, she'll make one.

Porcupines aren't good at hugging. But it's possible, and maybe a porcupine hug is even more rewarding than other hugs because it's so rare.

But most of our relationships are the sandpaper variety. We grit against each other. Sometimes we rub each other the wrong way. But in the end, we see our rough edges smoothed, the sharp corners rounded, and the natural beauty of wood grain showing through.

Sandpaper is a teacher, a friend, a parent—anyone who molds you, sometimes a little painfully, into a more useful form.

Ordinary people with ordinary relationships seldom walk uncluttered paths of

Sandpaper and Porcupines

happiness. There is the porcupine prickle and the sandpaper rub. Yet each brings its own reward.

God knows people don't live in easy harmony. That's why the apostle Paul gave instructions to the church at Rome on how to get along with a wide variety of ordinary people.

1. Speak briefly about one of your relationships that fits the sandpaper or porcupine description.

1. Encourage a brief response from each person but watch the clock in order to allow adequate time for the rest of the study. Be alert to keep the conversation from degenerating into gossip.

Read aloud Romans 12:9–13.

2. Find as many commands as you can in these verses. How can each one create a sense of belonging among Christians?

2. Your group should note the commands verbally, then discuss how each contributes to unity among believers. It will help your discussion if some give examples from their own experience about how following one of these commands gave them a sense of belonging.

3. Examine each of the six phrases in verses 11 and 12. What does each one mean?

3. Use the discussion of this question to lay groundwork for question 4. These spiritual traits will become more concrete if a few students outline examples of what a person who exhibits that trait would do. "A person who is not lacking in zeal would . . ."

Study 11

4. Use this question to tie together all of the paragraph.

4. How might developing the spiritual resources of verses 11 and 12 help believers accomplish the practical work of verses 9, 10, and 13?

Read aloud Romans 12:14–21.

5. Your group members should see themselves in the context described here. To distinguish between the first and last parts, notice that the first speaks of an emotional response to this setting, while the last calls for specific actions.

5. Look at the seven commands in verses 14–16. If you belonged to a group of people who practiced these standards, how would it make you feel?

What would your obligation be to such a group?

What practical benefits could you expect to receive from it?

6. Use verses 9–16 to discuss this action-based view of love.

6. Look again at the introductory statement to these verses, "Love must be sincere." How does the passage this far help you define sincere love?

Sandpaper and Porcupines

7. List the "do nots" of verses 16, 17, 19, and 21. Examine the negative and then the positive side to each of these statements. In what ways does each balance the other?

Note: Burning coals on the head!? F. F. Bruce interprets Paul's use of this ancient proverb, "'Treat your enemy kindly, for this may make him ashamed and lead to his repentance.' In other words, the best way to get rid of an enemy is to turn him into a friend, and so 'overcome evil with good' (verse 21)."

8. Verse 21 speaks a mandate for action. In what sense do you think that good is a power to overcome evil?

9. Think of your relationship with a friend, parent, brother, sister, teacher, or employer. (Choose one.) If you were to follow verses 18 and 21 in that relationship, what changes would you have to make in your own actions?

A Quote to Remember:
Do not be overcome by evil, but overcome evil with good. *Romans 12:21*

7. Your group should notice that these commands of "do not" lead not to inaction, but to action—and that the action of good is stronger than the evil it overcomes.

8. The passage does not speak of a soft fluffy "being good" that overlooks problems. Instead, it outlines positive good actions. Your students may find examples of this power that good can extend over evil throughout the passage. You can use these examples as stepping stones into a discussion of the general principle.

9. Allow time for as many as are willing to address this question. What repair work does it suggest on your own relationships?

If it seems appropriate, close your time together with brief sentence prayers of commitment in these steps toward healing in relationships.